Mastering AI with Prompts

Building Production-Ready Large Language Models

Fine-Tuning, Prompting, and Advanced Techniques to Develop Robust and Reliable Artificial intelligence Systems

---

Jamie T. Clinton

TABLE OF CONTENT

Introduction

Artificial Intelligence (AI) has rapidly transformed from a futuristic concept into a central force shaping the modern world. Its applications span industries, from healthcare to finance, education to entertainment. At the heart of this transformation lies an innovation that has revolutionized how machines process and generate human-like language: Large Language Models (LLMs). These models, powered by advanced neural networks, represent a monumental leap in our ability to interact with technology.

The history of AI is a tale of progress fueled by human ingenuity and perseverance. Early computer scientists dreamed of machines that could emulate human thought, but their capabilities were rudimentary.

In the mid-20th century, algorithms began to emerge that could perform basic problem-solving tasks.

The advent of machine learning in the 1980s and 1990s allowed systems to improve through experience, setting the stage for the explosion of data-driven AI in the 21st century. Neural networks, a concept inspired by the human brain, became the foundation of this new wave. With them came the advent of transformers, a breakthrough architecture introduced in 2017 that paved the way for the development of LLMs.

Models like GPT, BERT, and their successors have since captured the imagination of researchers and practitioners alike, pushing the boundaries of what machines can achieve.

Large Language Models have become a cornerstone of the AI revolution. Their ability to understand, generate, and manipulate human language has far-reaching implications.

These models have been integrated into chatbots, virtual assistants, automated content creation tools, and even medical diagnosis systems.

Their capacity to handle vast amounts of information and respond with nuanced, contextually aware outputs makes them indispensable in today's AI-driven landscape. LLMs are not just tools—they're enablers of innovation, enhancing productivity and enabling new possibilities across industries.

This book, *Mastering AI with Prompts: Building Production-Ready Large Language Models*, is crafted for those who wish to harness the power of these groundbreaking models. Whether you are an engineer aiming to develop cutting-edge AI systems, an enthusiast exploring the potentials of LLMs, or a decision-maker seeking to understand how to integrate AI into your organization, this book is for you.

The purpose here is to bridge the gap between theory and practice. By delving into fine-tuning, prompting, and advanced techniques, we provide actionable insights that will empower readers to build reliable, production-ready AI systems.

The challenge with LLMs often lies in understanding their complexities and applying them effectively in real-world scenarios. This book demystifies those complexities, offering a practical guide to mastering the tools and techniques essential for working with LLMs. By grounding theoretical concepts in practical applications, we ensure that the knowledge shared is not just insightful but immediately usable. From crafting effective prompts to fine-tuning models for specific tasks and deploying them at scale, this book provides a comprehensive roadmap.

As you journey through these pages, you will find a structured yet fluid narrative that unfolds seamlessly.

Each chapter builds on the last, taking you deeper into the fascinating world of LLMs. From understanding their foundational principles to exploring advanced applications, you will gain a holistic view of what it takes to master these powerful tools. This book is not just a technical manual; it is a guide to innovation, showing you how to unlock the potential of AI in a way that is both transformational and practical.

The chapters that follow are designed to cater to a diverse audience. Engineers will find the technical depth they need to refine their skills. AI enthusiasts will appreciate the accessible explanations and practical examples that demystify complex concepts. Decision-makers will gain a strategic understanding of how to deploy LLMs effectively within their organizations.

Together, these perspectives make this book a comprehensive resource, bridging the gap between diverse professional needs.

As you proceed, expect a journey through the fascinating evolution of LLMs, insights into their transformative potential, and hands-on strategies to apply them effectively.

This book begins with an exploration of the history and development of LLMs, setting the stage for a deeper dive into their technical intricacies. Later chapters will guide you through fine-tuning techniques, the art of crafting effective prompts, and strategies for deployment in production environments. Along the way, you'll encounter real-world case studies and practical examples that bring these concepts to life.

By the end of this book, you will not only understand how LLMs work but also possess the skills and knowledge to apply them in impactful ways. The ultimate goal is to empower you to innovate, leveraging AI to solve real-world problems and seize emerging opportunities.

Whether you are taking your first steps in this domain or looking to enhance your expertise, this book offers something for everyone.

This is your gateway to the world of LLMs—a world where the boundaries of technology and creativity blur, and the possibilities are limited only by your imagination. Welcome to the journey of mastering AI with prompts. Let's explore, learn, and innovate together.

Chapter 1: Understanding Large Language Models

What Are LLMs?

Large Language Models (LLMs) have redefined how we interact with technology, unlocking capabilities that were once the stuff of science fiction. At their core, LLMs are advanced artificial intelligence systems designed to understand, process, and generate human language. Unlike traditional rule-based systems, which require explicit programming for each task, LLMs learn from vast datasets, enabling them to perform a wide array of language-related tasks.

From answering complex questions to generating creative content, their applications are as diverse as they are transformative.

The foundation of LLMs lies in a groundbreaking architecture called the transformer.

Introduced in 2017, the transformer architecture revolutionized natural language processing by introducing a mechanism known as self-attention. This mechanism enables the model to weigh the relevance of each word in a sentence relative to others, allowing it to generate contextually accurate and coherent responses. Transformers replaced older, less efficient models like recurrent neural networks, which struggled with long-range dependencies in text.

Another critical concept underpinning LLMs is tokenization. Before processing, text is broken down into smaller units called tokens, which may represent words, subwords, or even individual characters. These tokens are then fed into the model, which assigns probabilities to predict the next token in a sequence.

This probabilistic approach allows LLMs to generate text that is not only grammatically correct but also contextually appropriate. For example, when given a prompt like "The sky is," an LLM might predict the next token as "blue," drawing from patterns it has learned during training.

The transformative power of LLMs stems from their ability to generalize across tasks. Pretrained on massive datasets, these models develop a broad understanding of language, enabling them to tackle tasks ranging from sentiment analysis to code generation. Fine-tuning, a process where a model is adapted to specific tasks using additional, focused datasets, further enhances their versatility.

This dual capability—generalization through pretraining and specificity through fine-tuning—has made LLMs indispensable tools in fields as diverse as healthcare, customer service, and content creation.

The Evolution of LLMs

The journey of LLMs is a testament to the rapid advancements in artificial intelligence over the past few decades. Early attempts at language modeling were rudimentary, relying on simple statistical techniques. However, the introduction of neural networks marked a turning point, allowing models to capture more complex patterns in text.

The first significant milestone in the evolution of LLMs was the development of GPT-1 by OpenAI in 2018. This model demonstrated the potential of unsupervised pre training, where a model learns from unstructured text data without labeled examples. Building on this foundation, GPT-2 showcased the power of scaling, with a larger dataset and more parameters leading to substantial improvements in text generation quality.

In 2020, GPT-3 took the world by storm with its staggering 175 billion parameters, setting a new benchmark for language models. Its ability to generate human-like text with minimal prompts highlighted the transformative potential of LLMs. Beyond text, GPT-3 also demonstrated emergent capabilities in reasoning and problem-solving, further expanding the horizons of AI.

The evolution of LLMs didn't stop there. The introduction of multimodal models, which integrate text with other data types like images and videos, marked the next frontier. For instance, models like GPT-4 and OpenAI's DALL·E demonstrated how LLMs could be extended to process and generate content across multiple modalities. This development has opened up new possibilities, from interactive virtual assistants to advanced data analysis tools.

These advancements reflect a broader trend in AI: the shift from specialized models to general-purpose systems.

Multimodal capabilities are particularly promising, as they enable AI to understand and respond to information in a more human-like, holistic manner. This progression underscores the versatility and scalability of LLMs, making them invaluable assets in a rapidly evolving technological landscape.

Limitations and Challenges

Despite their remarkable capabilities, LLMs are not without their limitations. One of the most significant constraints is their reliance on context windows, which determine the amount of text the model can process at once. While modern LLMs can handle more tokens than their predecessors, they still face challenges with lengthy or complex inputs. This limitation can impact their performance in tasks requiring a deep understanding of extended contexts, such as analyzing long documents or generating detailed reports.

Another critical issue is the presence of biases in LLMs. Since these models learn from large datasets that often reflect societal biases, they can inadvertently perpetuate stereotypes or discriminatory perspectives. For instance, an LLM trained on biased data might generate outputs that reinforce harmful narratives. Addressing this challenge requires careful curation of training data, as well as post-training techniques to mitigate bias.

The computational demands of LLMs also pose a barrier to their widespread adoption. Training these models requires immense computational resources, often running into millions of dollars for state-of-the-art systems. Even after training, deploying LLMs at scale can be cost-prohibitive, necessitating specialized hardware and infrastructure.

This has led to concerns about the accessibility of these technologies, particularly for smaller organizations and individual researchers.

Ethical considerations further complicate the deployment of LLMs. Issues such as data privacy, misinformation, and accountability must be addressed to ensure the responsible use of these models. For example, an LLM used in healthcare must prioritize patient confidentiality, while one deployed in content generation must include safeguards against spreading false information.

While these challenges are significant, they are not insurmountable. Researchers and practitioners are actively exploring solutions, from developing more efficient architectures to implementing robust ethical guidelines. Advances in techniques like sparse training and model compression aim to reduce computational costs, making LLMs more accessible. Similarly, initiatives to improve data transparency and fairness are helping to address biases and build trust in AI systems.

Understanding these limitations is crucial for leveraging LLMs effectively. By acknowledging their constraints and working to mitigate them, we can unlock their full potential while minimizing risks. As LLMs continue to evolve, they offer not just a glimpse into the future of AI but also an opportunity to shape it responsibly and innovatively.

Chapter 2: Mastering Fine-Tuning for LLMs

The Importance of Fine-Tuning

Fine-tuning is one of the most critical processes in maximizing the potential of Large Language Models (LLMs). While these models are initially trained on massive datasets covering a wide range of topics, fine-tuning allows them to specialize in specific tasks, making their outputs more accurate, relevant, and contextually appropriate. This adaptability transforms LLMs from general-purpose tools into highly targeted solutions tailored to real-world applications.

At its core, fine-tuning involves taking a pretrained model and further training it on a smaller, domain-specific dataset.

This process helps the model refine its understanding of a particular subject or task. For example, an LLM fine-tuned on legal documents can become adept at generating contracts, summarizing case law, or providing legal advice. Similarly, fine-tuning on medical datasets can enable the model to assist in diagnosing conditions, summarizing patient notes, or generating research insights.

Fine-tuning also addresses some of the inherent limitations of general pretrained models. While these models are powerful, their broad training often results in outputs that may lack precision for niche or specialized tasks. Fine-tuning narrows the model's focus, enhancing its ability to generate relevant responses for specific use cases.

For instance, a customer service chatbot fine-tuned on a company's support tickets will perform significantly better at resolving customer queries compared to a general-purpose chatbot.

Applications of fine-tuning span various industries. In the financial sector, fine-tuned LLMs are used for tasks like fraud detection, portfolio analysis, and automated financial reporting.

In education, they assist in personalized learning by generating tailored content for students based on their progress and needs. Fine-tuning is also instrumental in content creation, enabling models to adopt specific writing styles, adhere to brand guidelines, or produce specialized content such as technical manuals or creative narratives.

Techniques for Effective Fine-Tuning

The success of fine-tuning largely depends on the quality of the data and the techniques employed during the process. Data curation and preprocessing are foundational steps. The dataset used for fine-tuning must be clean, relevant, and representative of the task at hand.

This involves removing noise, filtering out irrelevant information, and ensuring consistency in formatting. For example, fine-tuning a model for customer service might require extracting high-quality examples of resolved tickets and organizing them into structured inputs and outputs.

Preprocessing often includes tokenization, where text is broken down into tokens that the model can process. Ensuring that the tokenization process aligns with the model's architecture is crucial for optimal performance. Additionally, augmenting the dataset with variations of common scenarios can improve the model's generalization capabilities, helping it handle a wider range of inputs.

Choosing the right optimization parameters and frameworks is another critical aspect of effective fine-tuning. Parameters such as learning rate, batch size, and the number of training epochs must be carefully selected to balance performance and computational efficiency. A learning rate that is too high may lead to overfitting, while one that is too low could result in underfitting. Batch size, which determines the number of samples processed before updating the model, also affects the model's ability to generalize.

Several frameworks and tools simplify the fine-tuning process. Libraries like Hugging Face's Transformers and OpenAI's API offer user-friendly interfaces for training and deploying fine-tuned models. These frameworks often include pretrained models, making it easier to fine-tune without starting from scratch. For instance, Hugging Face provides tools for fine-tuning GPT-based models with minimal code, enabling developers to focus on their specific tasks rather than the underlying complexities of the model.

Another advanced technique is transfer learning, where knowledge gained from one task is applied to another.

This approach can significantly reduce the amount of data and computation required for fine-tuning. For example, a model pre trained on general medical texts can be fine-tuned on a smaller dataset of dermatology reports to specialize in skin-related conditions.

Regular evaluation and validation are essential throughout the fine-tuning process. Metrics like accuracy, precision, recall, and F1 scores provide insights into the model's performance and help identify areas for improvement. Cross-validation, where the dataset is split into training and validation sets, ensures that the model is tested on unseen data, reducing the risk of overfitting.

Real-World Applications

The impact of fine-tuning becomes evident when examining real-world case studies. Consider the example of a healthcare provider that uses an LLM to analyze electronic health records (EHRs).

By fine-tuning the model on anonymized patient data, the provider can automate the generation of discharge summaries, saving time for healthcare professionals and improving patient care. The fine-tuned model is trained to identify key details from EHRs, such as diagnoses, treatments, and follow-up instructions, ensuring the summaries are both accurate and concise.

In another case, a legal tech company fine-tuned an LLM on thousands of legal briefs and court decisions. The resulting model could draft case summaries, suggest legal arguments, and even predict case outcomes with high accuracy. This innovation not only streamlined workflows but also reduced costs for clients by automating repetitive legal tasks.

In the realm of content creation, a media company fine-tuned an LLM to generate personalized newsletters for its subscribers.

By training the model on user preferences and historical data, it could produce tailored content that resonated with individual readers. This personalization increased engagement rates and strengthened the company's relationship with its audience.

The field of customer service also showcases the versatility of fine-tuning. A global e-commerce company fine-tuned an LLM on its support logs to create a chatbot capable of resolving common customer issues. The chatbot, trained to understand the company's specific products and policies, delivered accurate and timely responses, reducing the burden on human support agents and improving customer satisfaction.

Fine-tuning is not just about improving model performance; it's about unlocking the potential of LLMs to address specific challenges in innovative ways.

By leveraging curated data, advanced techniques, and robust frameworks, fine-tuning transforms LLMs into powerful tools capable of driving efficiency, accuracy, and value across industries.

Chapter 3: The Power of Prompt Engineering

Introduction to Prompting

Prompt engineering is one of the most effective techniques for unlocking the full potential of Large Language Models (LLMs). Prompts serve as the interface through which users interact with these models, providing the necessary context and instructions to generate meaningful and accurate outputs. The art of crafting effective prompts has become a cornerstone of working with LLMs, as even minor adjustments to a prompt can dramatically influence the quality of the model's responses.

At its core, prompting is about communication—how to clearly and efficiently convey what you want the model to do.

Prompts can range from simple one-line instructions to elaborate multi-sentence scenarios.

For example, asking a model to "Summarize the following text" is a basic prompt, while creating a detailed setup like "You are a financial advisor. Analyze the risks and opportunities in the following business proposal" represents a more advanced prompt. The ability of LLMs to understand and execute such instructions hinges on the clarity and structure of the prompt.

The importance of prompting lies in its ability to shape the behavior of the model. Well-crafted prompts can guide the model to focus on specific aspects of a task, ensuring relevance and accuracy in its responses. For example, in customer service applications, a clear and specific prompt might ensure the model provides concise and empathetic responses to user inquiries.

In contrast, poorly designed prompts can lead to irrelevant, vague, or even misleading outputs, undermining the effectiveness of the model.

Prompting techniques can be broadly categorized into basic and advanced approaches. Basic techniques involve straightforward instructions, often used for simple tasks like summarization or text completion. For instance, asking the model to "Generate a headline for this article" is a basic prompt. Advanced techniques, on the other hand, involve multi-step instructions, role-based scenarios, or even contextual setups that provide the model with detailed guidance.

For example, prompting the model to "Act as a teacher explaining the concept of gravitational force to a 10-year-old" employs an advanced technique by defining a specific role and audience.

Designing Effective Prompts

Crafting effective prompts requires a strategic approach. The goal is to make the prompt as clear, concise, and contextually relevant as possible. A well-designed prompt provides the model with all the necessary information to generate a high-quality response while avoiding ambiguity or unnecessary complexity.

One key strategy is to start with the end in mind. Define the desired outcome before drafting the prompt. For example, if the goal is to generate a list of creative marketing ideas, the prompt should explicitly state that requirement, such as "Provide five innovative marketing strategies for a new eco-friendly product." This specificity helps the model focus on the task and reduces the likelihood of irrelevant outputs.

Another important strategy is to use role-based instructions. Assigning a role to the model can help it adopt the perspective needed for the task.

For instance, prompting the model with "You are an experienced travel agent. Suggest a week-long itinerary for a family visiting Paris" guides the model to generate responses aligned with the expectations of that role.

Contextual information is also crucial. Providing background details or examples within the prompt can help the model better understand the task. For example, when asking for a summary, including the original text in the prompt ensures that the model focuses on the correct material. Similarly, when requesting creative writing, specifying the tone, style, or intended audience can improve the relevance and quality of the output.

Examples of effective prompts span a wide range of applications. In customer service, a prompt like "Respond to this customer query politely and professionally: 'I received a damaged product. What should I do next?'" ensures that the model generates a helpful and empathetic response.

In content creation, a prompt like "Write a blog introduction about the benefits of remote work, focusing on productivity and work-life balance" provides clear guidance on the topic and angle.

Evaluating and Optimizing Prompts

The effectiveness of a prompt often requires evaluation and iterative refinement. Metrics such as relevance, accuracy, and coherence can be used to assess the quality of the model's responses. If the output fails to meet expectations, analyzing the prompt for clarity and completeness can identify areas for improvement.

Iterative testing is a powerful approach to optimizing prompts. Start with an initial prompt and test it with the model. Evaluate the response and make adjustments to address any shortcomings. For example, if a prompt like "Explain quantum mechanics to a beginner" produces an overly technical response, refining the prompt to "Explain the basics of quantum mechanics to someone with no prior knowledge, using simple language and examples" can yield better results.

Another optimization technique involves experimenting with variations of the same prompt. Small changes in wording, structure, or additional context can significantly impact the quality of the output. For instance, rephrasing "Summarize this text" to "Provide a concise summary of this text, highlighting key points" might result in a more focused response.

It's also useful to test prompts across different scenarios and datasets to ensure consistency. A prompt that works well for one task might require adjustments for another. For example, a customer service prompt designed for handling complaints might need to be tailored differently for responding to product inquiries.

Tools and frameworks can aid in the evaluation and optimization of prompts. Platforms like OpenAI's GPT playground or Hugging Face's transformers library allow users to test and refine prompts interactively. These tools enable iterative experimentation, helping users identify the most effective prompts for their specific needs.

The process of evaluating and optimizing prompts is an ongoing effort. As tasks evolve or new use cases emerge, prompts may need to be revisited and refined. By continuously improving prompts, users can ensure that LLMs remain effective and aligned with their objectives.

Prompt engineering is both an art and a science. It combines creativity with systematic evaluation to maximize the capabilities of LLMs. Whether you're designing prompts for customer service, content creation, or specialized applications, the principles of clarity, relevance, and iterative refinement are key to achieving success. Through thoughtful prompt engineering, the full potential of LLMs can be harnessed to deliver transformative results across industries.

Chapter 4:
Retrieval-Augmented
Generation (RAG)

What Is RAG?

Retrieval-Augmented Generation (RAG) represents a powerful evolution in the capabilities of Large Language Models (LLMs). While LLMs are highly adept at generating coherent and contextually relevant text, their reliance on pre-trained knowledge limits their ability to provide up-to-date or domain-specific information. RAG bridges this gap by integrating LLMs with external data sources, enabling them to retrieve relevant information dynamically and generate responses enriched with real-time or specialized data.

At its core, RAG is a hybrid framework that combines the generative power of LLMs with the precision of information retrieval systems. Instead of relying solely on the model's internal knowledge, RAG systems query external databases, APIs, or knowledge bases to supplement the model's understanding.

This dual approach enhances the reliability and accuracy of the outputs, particularly for tasks requiring detailed or current information. For instance, a RAG system can retrieve the latest stock prices from a financial database and generate a comprehensive market analysis in real time.

The key advantage of RAG lies in its ability to expand the effective knowledge base of an LLM without the need for retraining. By connecting the model to external resources, RAG systems reduce the computational overhead of constantly updating the LLM itself. This makes it a cost-effective solution for applications that demand frequent access to fresh or evolving data.

Implementing RAG Systems

Building a RAG system involves creating a pipeline that seamlessly integrates data retrieval with text generation. The first step is setting up the retrieval mechanism. This typically involves identifying and indexing the external data sources relevant to the task. These sources can include structured databases, document repositories, or even web APIs. Tools like Elasticsearch, FAISS (Facebook AI Similarity Search), or vector databases are commonly used to enable efficient data retrieval.

Once the data sources are indexed, the system needs a mechanism to query them effectively. This is often done using embeddings, which represent text as numerical vectors in a multi-dimensional space. Embeddings enable semantic search, where the system retrieves data based on meaning rather than exact keyword matches.

For example, a query about "climate change policies" can retrieve documents discussing "global warming regulations" due to the semantic similarity between the terms.

After retrieving the relevant data, the next step is integrating it with the LLM. This involves combining the retrieved information with the user's input prompt and feeding it into the model. The challenge here is ensuring that the additional context is formatted in a way that the LLM can process effectively. Techniques like template-based formatting or hierarchical input structures can help achieve this.

Ensuring consistency and accuracy in outputs is a critical part of implementing RAG systems. The retrieved data must be accurate and relevant to the query, as errors at this stage can propagate into the generated response. Regularly updating the indexed data sources and employing validation mechanisms can help maintain data integrity.

Additionally, feedback loops can be used to refine the retrieval process based on user interactions, improving the system's performance over time.

Applications of RAG

RAG has a wide range of applications across industries, offering solutions for tasks that require both contextual understanding and precise information retrieval. In customer support, RAG systems can enhance chatbots by enabling them to pull information from product documentation, FAQs, and support tickets. This allows the chatbot to provide accurate and detailed answers, reducing the need for human intervention.

In research, RAG can streamline the process of literature reviews or data analysis. By retrieving relevant academic papers, reports, or datasets, RAG systems help researchers quickly access the information they need.

For example, a RAG-powered tool can assist a scientist studying renewable energy by retrieving the latest research on solar panel efficiency and summarizing key findings.

Automation is another area where RAG excels. Businesses can use RAG systems to automate tasks like generating financial reports, summarizing legal documents, or creating personalized marketing content. For instance, a RAG system integrated with a financial database could generate monthly investment summaries for clients, complete with charts and data-driven insights.

Practical Example

To illustrate the implementation of a RAG system, let's consider building a tool for customer support. The goal is to create a chatbot that can answer queries about a company's products using information from a knowledge base.

1. **Set Up Data Sources**: Start by compiling a knowledge base of product manuals, FAQs, and past customer support tickets. Index this data using a tool like Elasticsearch or FAISS to enable efficient retrieval.

2. **Develop Embeddings**: Use a pre-trained embedding model to convert the indexed documents into vector representations. This allows the system to perform semantic searches based on user queries.

3. **Build the Query System**: Implement a query mechanism that takes user input, converts it into an embedding, and retrieves the most relevant documents from the knowledge base.

4. **Integrate with the LLM**: Combine the retrieved documents with the user query to create an enriched input prompt. For example, if a user asks, "How do I reset my device?" the prompt

might include relevant sections from the product manual.

5. **Generate the Response**: Feed the enriched prompt into the LLM to generate a response. Ensure that the response incorporates the retrieved information while maintaining coherence and relevance.

6. **Validate and Improve**: Test the system with a variety of queries to identify areas for improvement. Use feedback loops to refine the retrieval process and improve the system's accuracy over time.

By following these steps, the resulting RAG system can provide users with detailed, accurate, and contextually relevant responses, significantly enhancing the quality of customer support.

RAG represents a transformative approach to leveraging LLMs for practical applications. By combining the strengths of information retrieval and text generation, it enables systems to deliver outputs that are both intelligent and informative. Whether in customer support, research, or automation, the potential of RAG is vast, offering solutions that bridge the gap between data and understanding.

Chapter 5: Deployment Strategies for LLMs

Challenges in Deployment

Deploying Large Language Models (LLMs) in real-world applications presents a unique set of challenges. While their capabilities are transformative, the complexities of scaling, ensuring reliability, and managing costs can create significant hurdles. These challenges must be addressed to ensure that LLMs perform effectively in production environments.

Scalability is one of the primary concerns in deployment. LLMs are computationally intensive, requiring substantial resources to process large volumes of requests. As user demand grows, systems must scale seamlessly to handle increased workloads without compromising performance. This often involves balancing computational efficiency with the ability to process high-throughput requests, especially in applications like chatbots or content generation platforms that operate in real time.

Reliability is another critical factor. LLMs must deliver consistent, accurate, and timely responses across a wide range of inputs. However, achieving this level of reliability can be challenging, as models may occasionally produce unexpected or irrelevant outputs. Ensuring uptime and preventing system failures also require robust infrastructure and failover mechanisms to minimize disruptions.

Cost considerations play a significant role in the feasibility of deploying LLMs. Training these models is resource-intensive, but even after deployment, maintaining the infrastructure to support them can be expensive.

Organizations must carefully manage resources to optimize performance while controlling operational costs. For smaller companies or startups, these financial challenges can be particularly prohibitive.

Preparing LLMs for Production

Before deploying LLMs into production, thorough preparation is essential. A key decision involves selecting the right infrastructure, which can significantly impact performance, scalability, and cost-effectiveness. Organizations typically choose between cloud-based, on-premises, or hybrid setups, depending on their specific needs.

Cloud-based solutions offer flexibility and scalability, allowing organizations to dynamically adjust resources based on demand. Providers like AWS, Google Cloud, and Azure offer pre-configured environments optimized for machine learning workloads.

These platforms reduce the need for upfront investment in hardware and simplify scaling, making them a popular choice for many deployments.

On-premises setups, while more resource-intensive to establish, provide greater control over data and infrastructure. This option is often preferred by organizations that handle sensitive information, such as healthcare or financial data, where compliance and security are critical. On-premises solutions allow organizations to tailor infrastructure to their specific requirements, though they require significant technical expertise to maintain.

Hybrid setups combine the strengths of both approaches, enabling organizations to leverage the scalability of cloud services for general workloads while maintaining sensitive operations on-premises.

This configuration provides a balanced approach, particularly for businesses with diverse requirements.

Beyond infrastructure, preparing LLMs for production involves extensive testing and optimization. Performance benchmarks should be established to evaluate the model's speed, accuracy, and scalability under various conditions. Stress testing ensures that the system can handle peak loads without degradation, while user simulations help identify potential bottlenecks.

Best Practices for Deployment

Deploying LLMs effectively requires adherence to best practices to ensure smooth operation and optimal performance. Monitoring is a critical aspect, providing real-time insights into the system's health and performance. Tools like Prometheus, Grafana, or cloud-native monitoring services can track metrics such as latency, throughput, and error rates.

Proactive monitoring helps identify and resolve issues before they impact users.

Error tracking is equally important, as even well-trained models can occasionally produce incorrect or unexpected outputs. Logging and analyzing these errors allow teams to identify patterns and refine the model or its inputs. Implementing a feedback loop where user interactions inform model adjustments can significantly improve performance over time.

Regular updates are essential to maintain the relevance and accuracy of LLMs. Language and knowledge evolve, and models must be periodically fine-tuned or retrained on updated datasets to remain effective. Automated pipelines for data ingestion, preprocessing, and retraining can streamline this process, reducing downtime and manual effort.

Integration with content filtering mechanisms is another best practice, particularly for applications where inappropriate or harmful content could be generated. Safeguards like toxicity filters or pre-defined response constraints help ensure that the outputs align with ethical and organizational standards.

Ethics and Security

Ethics and security considerations are paramount when deploying LLMs, as these systems can have far-reaching implications for users and society. Addressing biases is a key challenge, as LLMs trained on large datasets often inherit biases present in the data. These biases can manifest in harmful or discriminatory outputs, undermining trust in the system. Implementing bias mitigation strategies during training and fine-tuning, as well as post-deployment monitoring, can help address this issue.

Ensuring privacy is another critical aspect. LLMs often process sensitive user data, making it essential to safeguard this information against unauthorized access or misuse.

Encryption, secure APIs, and strict access controls are fundamental to protecting data. Additionally, compliance with regulations like GDPR or HIPAA ensures that deployments meet legal and ethical standards.

Safeguarding data also involves preventing unintended information leaks. LLMs can sometimes generate outputs that inadvertently reveal sensitive information, especially if they have been fine-tuned on proprietary datasets. Implementing safeguards to monitor and validate outputs before they reach users can mitigate these risks.

Security concerns extend beyond data protection. Deploying LLMs at scale makes them potential targets for malicious actors, such as adversarial attacks or misuse of the system's capabilities. For instance, an attacker might attempt to manipulate the model's inputs to produce harmful outputs.

Robust security measures, including input validation, anomaly detection, and regular security audits, are essential to defend against such threats.

Building trust is a critical component of ethical deployment. Transparent communication about the model's capabilities, limitations, and decision-making processes fosters user confidence. For example, making it clear when a user is interacting with an AI system rather than a human can enhance trust while aligning with ethical standards.

Deploying LLMs into production is a complex process that requires careful planning, robust infrastructure, and a commitment to ethical practices. From addressing scalability and reliability challenges to ensuring data security and mitigating biases, every aspect must be meticulously managed to achieve successful outcomes.

By adhering to best practices and prioritizing ethics, organizations can harness the transformative power of LLMs while minimizing risks and fostering trust in these powerful technologies.

Chapter 6: Advanced Techniques in LLM Development

Cutting-Edge Fine-Tuning Methods

The field of fine-tuning Large Language Models (LLMs) has evolved significantly, introducing advanced methods that push the boundaries of their capabilities. One such breakthrough is low-rank adaptation (LoRA), which has become a cornerstone for efficient and scalable fine-tuning. Traditional fine-tuning involves adjusting all the parameters of a pretrained model, which can be computationally expensive and resource-intensive.

LoRA, in contrast, updates only a subset of parameters, focusing on low-rank matrices that capture task-specific information.

This drastically reduces the computational overhead while maintaining or even improving performance on specialized tasks.

Another cutting-edge technique is parameter-efficient fine-tuning, which leverages adapters—small, trainable modules inserted into a pretrained model. Adapters allow for task-specific customization without altering the core model, enabling seamless switching between different tasks. This approach is particularly valuable for organizations that need a single model to handle multiple use cases, such as customer support, sentiment analysis, and content creation.

Prompt-tuning is another innovation that has gained traction. Unlike traditional fine-tuning, which modifies the model's weights, prompt-tuning adjusts the prompts fed into the model to guide its behavior.

This technique is highly efficient, as it requires minimal additional computation and can be applied to multiple tasks without retraining the model. For instance, a healthcare application might use a prompt like "You are a doctor. Summarize this patient's symptoms and suggest potential treatments," tailoring the model's output without altering its underlying structure.

These advanced methods not only enhance the efficiency of fine-tuning but also open up new possibilities for leveraging LLMs in resource-constrained environments. By reducing computational costs and increasing flexibility, they make LLMs accessible to a broader audience, fostering innovation across industries.

Multi-Modal LLMs

As the field of artificial intelligence advances, the integration of multiple modalities—such as text, images, and videos—into a single model has become a pivotal goal. Multi-modal LLMs are designed to process and generate outputs that combine these diverse data types, unlocking capabilities that were previously unattainable.

The architecture of multi-modal models often builds on the transformer framework, extending it to handle inputs from different modalities. For example, a multi-modal LLM might use separate encoders for text and images, followed by a shared decoder that synthesizes information from both sources. This approach enables the model to understand and generate rich, contextually relevant outputs that incorporate visual and textual elements.

Applications of multi-modal LLMs are vast and transformative. In healthcare, these models can analyze medical images alongside patient records, providing holistic insights for diagnosis and treatment planning.

In e-commerce, multi-modal systems enhance product recommendations by combining user reviews with product images and videos. Creative industries also benefit, as multi-modal LLMs can generate visual and textual content, such as designing marketing materials or crafting immersive storytelling experiences.

One notable example of a multi-modal LLM is OpenAI's CLIP, which pairs images with textual descriptions to create a model capable of understanding visual concepts in natural language. Similarly, DALL·E demonstrates the ability to generate high-quality images from textual prompts, showcasing the potential of multi-modal integration. These innovations highlight the growing importance of multi-modal models in addressing complex, real-world challenges.

Despite their promise, multi-modal LLMs face unique challenges. Aligning different modalities requires sophisticated techniques to ensure that the model accurately captures relationships between text, images, and videos. Additionally, the computational demands of training and deploying multi-modal models are substantial, necessitating advances in hardware and optimization algorithms.

Continuous Learning

One of the key challenges in deploying LLMs is ensuring that they remain relevant and effective as data and contexts evolve. Continuous learning, also known as online learning or incremental learning, addresses this issue by enabling models to adapt dynamically to new information without requiring retraining from scratch.

Continuous learning involves updating the model incrementally with fresh data while preserving its existing knowledge. This approach is particularly valuable in domains where information changes rapidly, such as news, finance, and healthcare.

For instance, a news aggregation platform might use continuous learning to ensure its LLM stays up to date with the latest developments, providing accurate and timely summaries for users.

To implement continuous learning, organizations typically use techniques such as replay buffers, where a portion of past data is retained and combined with new data during updates. This helps prevent catastrophic forgetting, a phenomenon where the model loses previously learned information when exposed to new data. Another technique is knowledge distillation, where a smaller, updated model is trained to mimic the outputs of a larger, pretrained model, effectively transferring knowledge while incorporating new information.

The benefits of continuous learning extend beyond maintaining model accuracy. It also reduces the costs and time associated with full-scale retraining, making it a practical solution for long-term deployment.

Moreover, continuous learning fosters personalization by allowing models to adapt to individual user preferences over time. For example, a recommendation system might refine its suggestions based on a user's evolving interests, improving engagement and satisfaction.

However, continuous learning is not without challenges. Ensuring data quality is paramount, as incorporating noisy or biased data can degrade model performance. Additionally, computational efficiency must be maintained, as frequent updates can strain resources. Addressing these challenges requires robust data pipelines, efficient update mechanisms, and careful monitoring to balance adaptability with stability.

Advanced techniques in LLM development, including cutting-edge fine-tuning methods, multi-modal integration, and continuous learning, are driving the next wave of innovation in artificial intelligence.

These approaches enhance the versatility, efficiency, and relevance of LLMs, enabling them to tackle increasingly complex tasks and adapt to ever-changing environments. By leveraging these techniques, organizations can unlock new possibilities, creating AI systems that are not only powerful but also resilient and responsive to the demands of the modern world.

Chapter 7: Building Reliable and Robust AI Systems

Ensuring Robustness

Building reliable and robust AI systems starts with ensuring that the underlying Large Language Models (LLMs) perform effectively under diverse conditions. Robustness refers to the model's ability to handle a variety of inputs, including edge cases and unexpected scenarios, without failure. This is critical for maintaining user trust and ensuring that AI systems provide accurate and meaningful outputs in real-world applications.

Testing and validation are the cornerstone techniques for ensuring robustness in LLMs. Rigorous testing involves subjecting the model to a broad range of inputs, from typical cases to outliers that may challenge its understanding or generate ambiguous results.

Automated testing pipelines can evaluate the model's responses against predefined benchmarks, checking for accuracy, relevance, and consistency. Validation, on the other hand, involves comparing the model's outputs with ground truth data or human annotations to ensure alignment with expectations.

Simulating edge cases is an important aspect of robustness testing. Edge cases are scenarios that fall outside the typical data the model was trained on, such as highly technical jargon, slang, or incomplete queries. For instance, an LLM deployed in customer service should handle misspelled words or poorly phrased questions effectively. To prepare the model for these scenarios, synthetic datasets that mimic edge cases can be created and incorporated into the testing process.

Techniques like adversarial testing further enhance robustness by deliberately introducing challenging inputs to evaluate how the model responds under pressure.

This might include prompts designed to confuse the model or highlight potential biases. By identifying weaknesses through adversarial testing, developers can refine the model's architecture, training data, or post-processing steps to mitigate vulnerabilities.

Reliability in Production

Reliability is a fundamental requirement for deploying LLMs in production environments. Users expect consistent performance, minimal downtime, and accurate outputs, making it essential to implement strategies that ensure uptime and fail-safe mechanisms.

One of the key strategies for reliability is redundancy. Deploying multiple instances of an LLM across different servers or geographic locations helps ensure that the system remains operational even if one instance fails.

Load balancers can distribute traffic among these instances, preventing overloads and maintaining response times during peak demand.

Fail-safe mechanisms are equally important. These mechanisms enable the system to gracefully handle errors or unexpected conditions without disrupting the user experience. For example, if the LLM encounters an input it cannot process, a fallback system—such as a predefined response or escalation to a human operator—can maintain continuity. Logging errors and exceptions in real-time provides valuable insights for troubleshooting and improving the system over time.

Scalability is another critical aspect of reliability. LLMs must be able to handle varying workloads efficiently, from low-traffic periods to sudden spikes in demand. This requires scalable infrastructure, such as cloud-based environments that allow dynamic allocation of resources.

Autoscaling ensures that the system can handle increased traffic without degradation in performance.

Monitoring tools play a vital role in maintaining reliability. Metrics such as response time, throughput, and error rates provide a real-time view of the system's performance. Alerts can be configured to notify operators of anomalies, enabling rapid intervention to prevent or resolve issues.

Guardrails for LLMs

Implementing guardrails is essential for ensuring that LLMs produce safe, relevant, and appropriate outputs. These guardrails serve as a layer of control that moderates the model's behavior, particularly in applications where generating harmful or misleading content could have serious consequences.

Content filtering is one of the most effective guardrails for LLMs.

By applying filters to the model's outputs, developers can prevent the generation of inappropriate, biased, or harmful content. These filters use predefined rules or machine learning models trained to detect and block problematic outputs. For instance, a chatbot designed for educational purposes might filter out offensive language or misinformation.

Routing mechanisms add another layer of control by directing specific queries to the most appropriate model or response system. This is particularly useful in multi-purpose applications where the LLM may not be the best tool for every task. For example, a customer service system might route technical support queries to a specialized database or human agent while using the LLM for general inquiries.

Moderation ensures that the system adheres to ethical guidelines and user expectations. Human-in-the-loop (HITL) moderation is a common approach, where human reviewers oversee the model's outputs and intervene when necessary. This is especially important in applications where accuracy and sensitivity are critical, such as legal or medical contexts. HITL moderation also provides feedback that can be used to refine the model and improve its performance over time.

Proactive guardrails involve designing the model and its deployment environment with safety in mind. For example, incorporating response templates or restricting the model's output to specific domains can reduce the risk of inappropriate or irrelevant responses. Similarly, employing ethical AI frameworks during development helps align the model's behavior with societal values and organizational standards.

Building reliable and robust AI systems requires a multi-faceted approach that combines rigorous testing, strategic deployment practices, and proactive safeguards.

By ensuring robustness through thorough validation and testing, organizations can prepare LLMs to handle diverse scenarios effectively.

Reliability in production is achieved through redundancy, scalability, and continuous monitoring, ensuring that systems remain operational and responsive under varying conditions. Finally, implementing guardrails such as content filtering, routing, and moderation adds a crucial layer of safety, enhancing user trust and protecting against potential risks.

Together, these strategies enable organizations to deploy LLMs that are not only powerful but also dependable, secure, and aligned with ethical standards.

Chapter 8: Case Studies and Practical Applications

Successful LLM Deployments

Large Language Models (LLMs) have been successfully deployed across numerous industries, demonstrating their transformative potential in solving complex problems, streamlining workflows, and creating innovative solutions. These real-world examples showcase the versatility and value of LLMs when effectively applied.

In the **healthcare sector**, LLMs have revolutionized how patient data is analyzed and utilized. For instance, medical institutions use LLMs to summarize patient records, extract critical information, and assist in diagnostics.

By fine-tuning models on anonymized datasets of electronic health records, healthcare providers have automated the creation of discharge summaries and treatment plans, reducing administrative burdens and improving patient care. LLMs are also used in medical research to generate insights from vast amounts of scientific literature, accelerating discoveries in fields like genetics and drug development.

The **financial industry** has leveraged LLMs to enhance fraud detection, portfolio management, and customer engagement. One prominent application involves using LLMs to analyze transaction data and identify patterns indicative of fraudulent activity. By integrating LLMs into their systems, financial institutions have improved detection rates while minimizing false positives.

In investment management, LLMs are used to analyze market trends and generate forecasts, enabling data-driven decision-making. Additionally, chatbots powered by LLMs provide personalized financial advice and support to customers, enhancing the user experience.

In **education**, LLMs have transformed personalized learning experiences. Online learning platforms deploy LLMs to generate custom study materials, quizzes, and explanations tailored to individual student needs. For example, an AI tutor might adapt its responses based on a student's knowledge level, ensuring concepts are explained at an appropriate depth. This personalization has significantly improved learning outcomes and engagement, particularly in subjects like mathematics and language learning.

The **retail and e-commerce sectors** have embraced LLMs for enhancing customer service and optimizing operations. Chatbots powered by LLMs handle customer inquiries, recommend products, and assist with order tracking, providing round-the-clock support.

Retailers also use LLMs to analyze customer reviews and feedback, gaining insights into consumer preferences and improving product offerings. In logistics, LLMs streamline supply chain operations by forecasting demand and optimizing inventory management.

Challenges and Lessons Learned

Despite these successes, deploying LLMs in real-world applications comes with its own set of challenges. One common issue is **data quality and availability**. For an LLM to perform effectively, it requires high-quality, domain-specific training data. In industries with limited or fragmented datasets, this can be a significant barrier. Organizations have addressed this by investing in data collection and curation efforts, ensuring that training datasets are representative and reliable.

Another challenge is **managing computational costs**. LLMs are resource-intensive, and deploying them at scale can strain infrastructure and budgets.

Companies have mitigated this by using efficient fine-tuning techniques, such as parameter-efficient tuning or transfer learning, which reduce the computational demands without compromising performance. Cloud-based solutions and scalable infrastructure have also been key in managing these costs.

Ethical concerns and biases present another hurdle. LLMs can inadvertently generate biased or inappropriate content, especially when trained on datasets that reflect societal biases. Organizations have tackled this by implementing robust content filtering mechanisms, conducting bias audits, and incorporating human oversight into deployment workflows.

Transparent communication with users about the model's capabilities and limitations has further helped build trust.

Lessons learned from successful deployments emphasize the importance of **iterative testing and feedback**. Regular evaluation and updates to the model ensure that it remains effective and relevant. Engaging end-users in the development process has also proven beneficial, as their feedback provides valuable insights into improving the system's usability and functionality.

Building Your First LLM-Based Application

Developing your first LLM-based application can seem daunting, but with a structured approach, the process becomes manageable and rewarding. Here is a practical step-by-step guide:

1. **Define Your Objective**: Begin by identifying the problem you want to solve and the specific tasks the LLM will perform. For instance, are you building a chatbot for customer service, or do you need a system to analyze financial reports? Clear objectives will guide the development process and help in selecting the right model and tools.

2. **Choose Your LLM**: Based on your objectives, select an appropriate LLM. Pretrained models like OpenAI's GPT, Hugging Face's Transformers, or Google's BERT provide powerful starting points. Consider factors such as the model's capabilities, licensing terms, and compatibility with your infrastructure.

3. **Prepare Your Data**: Gather and preprocess the data required for fine-tuning the model. Ensure that the dataset is clean, relevant, and representative of the tasks your

application will handle. For example, if you are building a customer service chatbot, curate a dataset of resolved support tickets and FAQs.

4. **Fine-Tune the Model**: Fine-tune the chosen LLM on your curated dataset to adapt it to your specific use case. Use frameworks like Hugging Face or OpenAI's API for this process. Fine-tuning enhances the model's performance by tailoring it to your domain.

5. **Develop the Application Interface**: Create an interface that connects users to the LLM. This could be a web app, a mobile app, or an API endpoint. Ensure that the interface is user-friendly and designed to streamline interactions with the model.

6. **Implement Guardrails**: Integrate mechanisms to filter content, moderate responses, and ensure ethical use. For instance, add content filters to prevent

inappropriate outputs and implement monitoring tools to track performance.

7. **Test and Iterate**: Conduct extensive testing to evaluate the application's performance under various conditions. Gather feedback from users and refine the system based on their input. Iterative improvements ensure that the application meets user expectations and performs reliably.

8. **Deploy and Monitor**: Deploy your application in a production environment, ensuring scalability and reliability. Use monitoring tools to track metrics such as response times, error rates, and user satisfaction. Regular updates and maintenance will keep the system relevant and effective.

By following these steps, you can build an LLM-based application that delivers value to users and meets your objectives. Whether you're developing a small prototype or a large-scale system, careful planning and execution are key to success.

Case studies and practical applications of LLMs highlight their immense potential to transform industries and solve real-world problems. From personalized education to automated customer support, these models offer innovative solutions that drive efficiency and improve user experiences.

By learning from successful deployments and overcoming challenges, you can harness the power of LLMs to create impactful applications. With a clear objective, robust data, and careful implementation, your first LLM-based application can pave the way for groundbreaking advancements in your field.

Chapter 9: The Future of AI and LLMs

Emerging Trends

The future of Artificial Intelligence (AI) and Large Language Models (LLMs) is being shaped by rapid advancements in technology, offering exciting possibilities that were once unimaginable. Among the most significant emerging trends are new architectures that improve efficiency, scalability, and adaptability. Models are becoming more modular, allowing components to be reused or replaced without retraining the entire system.

For example, advancements in sparsity techniques enable models to focus computational resources on the most relevant parts of a task, improving performance while reducing costs.

Emergent abilities in LLMs are another fascinating development.

As these models grow in size and complexity, they demonstrate capabilities that were not explicitly programmed or expected. These include complex reasoning, few-shot learning, and the ability to generalize across domains. These emergent abilities hint at a future where models can perform tasks that extend beyond their original design, unlocking new opportunities for innovation.

Generative AI continues to push boundaries, with models becoming increasingly capable of creating content across multiple modalities, such as text, images, and video. Multimodal models, like those that combine language with visual inputs, are paving the way for AI systems that can understand and generate rich, contextually relevant outputs.

This trend has vast implications, from immersive virtual environments to advanced decision-making tools.

The Expanding Role of AI

AI's influence is expanding rapidly across industries, reshaping how organizations operate and individuals interact with technology. In healthcare, AI is revolutionizing diagnostics, treatment planning, and patient management. LLMs are being used to analyze medical literature, assist in drug discovery, and provide personalized care recommendations, leading to more accurate and efficient healthcare delivery.

In education, AI is personalizing learning experiences by adapting content to individual needs. LLMs power virtual tutors that help students grasp complex concepts, while generative AI tools create engaging, interactive learning materials.

This transformation is bridging educational gaps and democratizing access to quality education worldwide.

The business sector is leveraging AI to optimize operations, enhance customer experiences, and drive innovation. From automating routine tasks to generating strategic insights from big data, AI is enabling companies to operate more efficiently and make informed decisions. In creative industries, LLMs are transforming content creation, enabling artists, writers, and designers to experiment and innovate in ways that were previously impossible.

Society at large is also feeling the transformative effects of AI. It is shaping how people communicate, access information, and engage with the world around them. Virtual assistants powered by LLMs are becoming integral to daily life, while AI-driven tools are empowering individuals to solve problems and express themselves creatively.

However, with this expansion comes the need for thoughtful consideration of AI's ethical implications, including fairness, accountability, and inclusivity.

Inspiring Innovation

The future of AI is not just about the technology itself but also about the people who will harness its potential to create meaningful change. Innovation in AI is driven by curiosity, creativity, and a willingness to explore uncharted territory. As the field evolves, there are countless opportunities for readers to contribute to this dynamic landscape.

For aspiring developers, creating novel applications of LLMs can lead to breakthroughs in various domains. By combining technical skills with domain knowledge, individuals can design AI systems that solve real-world problems, whether in healthcare, education, business, or the arts.

For instance, an entrepreneur might develop an AI-powered platform to streamline supply chain management, while an educator could create tools that make learning more accessible to underserved communities.

For researchers, the rapidly advancing field of AI presents opportunities to delve into fundamental questions about intelligence, language, and learning. By exploring new architectures, optimization techniques, or applications, researchers can push the boundaries of what AI systems can achieve. Collaborative efforts between academia, industry, and government can accelerate innovation, ensuring that advancements benefit society as a whole.

For the broader public, understanding and engaging with AI is increasingly important. As technology becomes more integrated into everyday life, individuals can benefit from learning how to use AI tools effectively and responsibly.

This engagement also empowers people to participate in discussions about AI's impact, shaping policies and practices that align with societal values.

Resources for Continuous Learning

Staying informed and skilled in the field of AI requires a commitment to continuous learning. Fortunately, there are abundant resources available to help readers stay ahead of the curve.

Books and Research Papers: Foundational texts like *Deep Learning* by Ian Goodfellow and advanced readings like *Attention Is All You Need* provide insights into the principles and innovations driving AI. Staying updated with research papers on platforms like arXiv helps readers track the latest developments.

Online Courses and Tutorials: Platforms like Coursera, edX, and Udemy offer courses on machine learning, deep learning, and AI applications. Specialized courses, such as those on Hugging Face's Transformers library, provide hands-on training with LLMs.

Communities and Forums: Engaging with AI communities fosters collaboration and knowledge sharing. Online forums like Reddit's r/MachineLearning, GitHub repositories, and discussion groups on Discord or Slack are valuable platforms for exchanging ideas and troubleshooting challenges.

AI Tools and Libraries: Experimenting with tools like TensorFlow, PyTorch, and Hugging Face helps readers gain practical experience. These libraries provide pre-built models and frameworks that simplify AI development and deployment.

Conferences and Workshops: Attending events like NeurIPS, ICML, and CVPR offers opportunities to network with experts, learn about cutting-edge research, and gain inspiration for future projects.

Open Source Contributions: Contributing to open-source projects enables readers to collaborate with the AI community while honing their skills. Platforms like GitHub host numerous projects where individuals can participate and learn.

The future of AI and LLMs is bright, brimming with possibilities that extend beyond our current imagination. From emerging trends in architectures and generative abilities to the expanding role of AI in industries and society, the potential for innovation is boundless. As readers explore these opportunities, they are encouraged to think creatively, collaborate widely, and approach AI with both curiosity and responsibility.

By leveraging the resources and insights shared in this book, readers can equip themselves to be active participants in shaping the AI landscape. Whether as developers, researchers, or informed citizens, their contributions will play a crucial role in ensuring that AI's future is both impactful and inclusive. Let this be a starting point for a journey of continuous learning and discovery, driving forward the extraordinary potential of AI.

Conclusion

The journey through this book has unraveled the fascinating world of Large Language Models (LLMs) and their transformative potential in artificial intelligence. From understanding the foundational concepts to exploring advanced techniques, you have gained insights into the architecture, capabilities, and applications of LLMs. Each chapter has built upon the last, providing a comprehensive view of how these powerful tools are reshaping industries and opening doors to innovation.

You began by delving into the basics, learning what LLMs are and how they work. The revolutionary transformer architecture, attention mechanisms, and tokenization laid the groundwork for understanding the intricate processes that enable these models to process and generate human-like language. The historical evolution of LLMs, from their early stages to cutting-edge multimodal capabilities, highlighted the rapid pace of innovation in this field.

Through the exploration of fine-tuning and prompt engineering, you discovered the art and science of tailoring LLMs to specific tasks. These techniques demonstrated how the versatility of LLMs could be harnessed to solve real-world problems, from healthcare to customer service, content creation to education. The chapter on Retrieval-Augmented Generation (RAG) showcased how LLMs could integrate with external data sources, extending their capabilities and ensuring their relevance in dynamic environments.

The challenges and strategies for deploying LLMs into production were laid bare, offering a roadmap for scalability, reliability, and ethical considerations. You learned about the importance of guardrails to ensure safety, the necessity of monitoring to maintain performance, and the value of continuous updates to keep models aligned with evolving data and expectations.

Advanced techniques and trends provided a glimpse into the future, from the emergence of new architectures and multimodal systems to the expanding role of AI in industries and society. Practical applications and case studies brought these concepts to life, illustrating the real-world impact of LLMs across diverse domains. The step-by-step guide to building your first LLM-based application empowered you to take actionable steps toward leveraging these technologies in your own projects.

Recap of Key Insights

This book has equipped you with the knowledge to navigate the complexities of LLMs, from foundational principles to practical applications. You've learned about the importance of robust testing, ethical considerations, and adaptive strategies that ensure models perform reliably in production. By understanding the capabilities and limitations of LLMs, you are now better prepared to harness their potential while addressing challenges responsibly.

Through the various examples, techniques, and methodologies explored in these chapters, you've gained a toolkit for working with LLMs effectively. Whether you are a developer fine-tuning a model, a decision-maker exploring AI integration, or a researcher pushing the boundaries of what LLMs can achieve, the insights shared here provide a solid foundation for success.

As you close this book, remember that this is not the end of the journey but the beginning of an exciting adventure. AI and LLMs are constantly evolving, presenting new challenges and opportunities at every turn.

Your curiosity, creativity, and commitment to learning will be the driving forces that enable you to innovate and make a meaningful impact in this field.

Take the next steps with confidence. Experiment with the tools and techniques you've learned. Engage with the AI community to share ideas, collaborate on projects, and stay informed about the latest advancements. Seek out new resources, attend workshops, and contribute to discussions that shape the future of AI.

Above all, approach your work with a sense of responsibility and purpose. AI has the power to transform lives and industries, but it also comes with ethical implications that demand careful consideration. By prioritizing fairness, inclusivity, and transparency, you can help ensure that the benefits of AI are shared widely and equitably.

The future of AI is in your hands. Whether you are building innovative applications, advancing research, or advocating for responsible practices, your efforts will shape the trajectory of this transformative technology. Embrace the possibilities, rise to the challenges, and let your journey in AI be one of exploration, discovery, and positive impact.

Thank you for embarking on this journey through the world of LLMs. The tools and insights you now possess are just the beginning. The possibilities are limitless, and the future is waiting. Go forth and make it extraordinary.